Candle Making

Step-by-Step Guide to Homemade Candles

Josephine Simon

Disclaimer and Terms of Use
Efforts have been made to ensure that the information in this book is accurate and complete. However, the author and the publisher do not warrant the accuracy of the information, text, and graphics contained within the book due to the rapidly changing nature of science, research, known and unknown facts, and internet. The author and the publisher do not hold any responsibility for errors, omissions, or contrary interpretation of the subject matter herein. This book is presented solely for motivational and informational purposes only. The publisher and author of this book does not control or direct users' actions and are not responsible for the information or content shared, harm and/or action of the book readers. The information herein is offered for informational purposes solely and is universal as so. The presentation of the information is without contract or any type of guarantee assurance.

ISBN: 9781077240308

Printed in the United States

CONTENTS

INTRODUCTION TO THE WORLD OF CANDLE MAKING

Do you love relaxing in a room lit by the soft glow of candlelight? Do you enjoy lingering in a candle store, smelling practically every candle as you try to pick the one that's the perfect gift for someone special? If so, you're not alone. Candles are a beautiful part of our lives, and many of us have a bit of an obsession with them.

Our love affair with candles has lasted a long time. Candles aren't the primary source of light nowadays, yet every household has them on hand. Candles give a glow, soft warmth and irresistible atmosphere to any room. There's a nuance that comes when you light a candle that you just can't get by switching on a bulb. Candles of different colors and scents serve as home decor, are lit during celebrations such as weddings and birthdays, and set the tone for romantic evenings and more. Even when nothing's going on, they lift the mood and provide a warm and soothing atmosphere in the home. They're a token of beauty that adds to the beauty of the whole house, and many of them have a beautiful scent as well. No matter what shape or color it is, a candle helps create a pleasant, happy environment.

We purchase a lot of things to make our homes look elegant and alluring, and there's no denying that candle shopping is an enjoyable pastime, but if you're anything like me, it doesn't take long before you start looking around and thinking about how you could probably make candles just like these yourself for a lot less money.

Candle making as a craft has become a popular, enjoyable pastime for people of all ages. It's perfect because it's so adaptable to personal preferences. You can begin your candle making adventures with simple projects like melt-and-pour container candles or try something more complex, like a molded, layered pillar with each layer having a distinct color and scent. You also have total control over the ingredients, so your homemade candles are going to contain far fewer chemicals and toxins than store-bought ones. There's no one-size-fits-all approach to candle making—you can create whatever your heart desires. Compared to other crafts, candle making is relatively easy to learn, and the startup costs can be based entirely on your budget.

Creativity, ease, and affordability—does it get any better than that? Not really, and chances are that once you start making your own candles, you'll never even think about purchasing online or off the shelf ever again.

Aside from a few basic materials, you really don't need much to get started with your candle making adventure other than a bit of knowledge and some tried-and-true techniques—and you'll get those from this book.

While candle making is a relatively straightforward process, there's an incredible amount of information that can be found about it. This book is intended to provide you with the basics that you need to know for creating your first candles. Once you have these basics mastered, you can then go on to learn more about advanced candle making techniques, including special additives, molds, and artistic touches.

Everyone can learn to make candles at home; it's only a matter of giving it some time and being creative. And when the candles are lit, they spread a calming effect which soothes your soul and makes you more comfortable in your surroundings. There are numerous variations to keep things interesting, including scents, types of wax, molds and much more. And while homemade candles are great decorations for your house, they're equally great as gifts for your friends and loved ones. It's a very kind, thoughtful gesture to gift homemade candles to someone you care about.

Are you ready to jump in and become acquainted with your new favorite hobby? Sit down, relax and light a candle as you read this book and prepare to start your candle making adventures. But first, let discover where candles originated and a brief history about candle making around the world.

A Brief History

Candles have been around for at least 5,000 years, and probably much longer; we can assume that people began using rudimentary candle-like light sources about the same time they began using fire. However, the earliest archeological evidence of modern candles dates back to about 3000 B.C. Candle holders from this period have been found in both Greece and Egypt.

Candles were used as the primary source of light in the earliest eras of human history. The ancient Egyptians initially lit their homes, palaces and temples with torches made from reeds and animal fat, but by the early third century BC they were using wick candles. The ancient Romans made candles by dipping rolls of papyrus into melted beeswax. They used those candles for lighting their houses, traveling at night, and certain religious ceremonies. In fact, candles saw ceremonial use in many ancient cultures; Hanukkah, the Jewish "Festival of Lights", first used candles in 165 BC.

Early Eastern civilizations also created wax candles out of locally available animals and plants. Chinese candles were molded from paper tubes wrapped around the wick, and the wax was made out of seeds and tree nuts. The ancient Indians were already cultivating cinnamon trees, and so they used cinnamon berries to create wax for their candles as well.

However, Europe became the primary locus of early modern candle making. Millennia-old pieces of candle wax have been discovered in France, but the Romans were the first Europeans to make wick candles.

Throughout the first millennium, most candles were made from beeswax, which is relatively soft and difficult to work with. It's not suitable for dipped candles, so before candle molds became common, beeswax candles usually had to be hand-formed. Beeswax is also rather scarce. Thus, candles during this period were so costly that they were effectively reserved for churches, monasteries and wealthy households.

Candles made from tallow (rendered animal fat) were introduced during the Middle Ages. By the 13th century, candle making was well established as a skilled trade in France and England, and many Europeans used tallow candles in their houses. Some candle makers, who were known as chandlers, owned shops where they made and sold candles. Others went from house to house making candles on site from saved animal fat.

Later on, women in the American colonies discovered that boiling the berries they used in candle making would make the wax smell better, burn more cleanly, and last longer. In the 18th century, tallow candles were supplanted by ones made from newly-discovered spermaceti (whale oil), which produced less smoke and a brighter light. It was also harder and would not deform due to changes in temperature.

In the early 1800s, Michel Chevreul discovered a technique for extracting stearic acid from fatty acids of animal origin. This led to the creation of stearin wax, which was the most reliable and durable candle wax to date. Stearin candles were harder and burned longer, and they quickly became very popular. Even now, many Europeans still prefer them.

Paraffin, though—white, almost odorless, smooth-burning and economical—has been the number one candle wax ever since it was first separated from petroleum in the 1850s. At around the same time, Joseph Morgan developed a machine for molding cylindrical candles automatically. The mechanism was easy to understand and eliminated the need for each candle to be hand-poured and hand-released from its mold. This process, which is still in use today, made candles much more affordable.

Nonetheless, they still couldn't compete with the electric light bulb, which was invented in the early 1880s. Candle use declined sharply as more and more homes were connected to the electrical grid. Still, candles continued to hold a place in homes—both for their romantic ambiance and for the occasions when the miracle of electricity let us down. For most of the 20th century, American candles made from a mixture of stearin and paraffin sold steadily but slowly.

In the mid–80s, candles became popular as household decorations. Soon they were widely being given as gifts and used to set the mood for special occasions. The revival of interest spurred candle makers to create different shapes, sizes and colors, which in turn attracted even more customers and prompted the first significant technological developments in the field for over a hundred years. In the early 90s, chemists developed a soybean wax which burned slower than paraffin, and palm wax made its debut in Europe. And somewhere around the mid to late 90s, the popularity of candles boomed once again—this time in the form of a hobby that captured the attention of people who wanted to try their own hand at the ancient art of candle making.

TYPES OF CANDLES

When you go candle shopping, what are you looking for? A certain color, or maybe the perfect floral or spice scent to fragrance your home? Most of the time, color and scent are secondary attributes for choosing candles. It's usually the shape and form that will capture your attention first.

Maybe you want a jar candle to place on the kitchen counter, or a set of beautiful pillars in different sizes as a centerpiece to grace your dining room table. Due to the variety of molds and containers available, the only real limit is your imagination. That said, most candles fall somewhere in the spectrum of the shapes and forms listed here.

- **Pillars** are thick candles that are able to stand on their own without the support of a container or candle holder. They are typically made from strong waxes such as paraffin, palm wax, and beeswax. Pillars range from 2–3 inches to 6 inches or more in diameter, and they can be quite tall. Larger pillar candles usually require multiple wicks to ensure even burning.

- **Tapers** are thin candles that require some type of support, such as a candlestick or candelabra. They're usually plain and relatively long, but they can be smaller and colored, too—like candles for a birthday cake. Since they're only supported at the base, tapers should be made from a firm wax like paraffin or beeswax so they don't droop. They can be formed either with a mold or by dipping.

- **Rolled** candles are made using sheets of pliable wax, most often beeswax. You can make both tapers and pillars this way, and since this method doesn't require any melting or pouring, it's a great way to go for beginning and younger candle makers.

- **Votives** are small candles, typically about 2½ inches high, that are burnt in cup-like glass candleholders. Since they don't need to support themselves, feel free to experiment with different combinations of waxes, like palm and beeswax, soy and palm wax, or blends of paraffin.

- **Tealights** are container candles that are even smaller than votives—about 1½ inches in diameter and much less in height. Tealights are often used in wax warmers and in some specially designed candle holder, but you can place them on a plate or on pretty much any other nonflammable surface. Tealights can be made out of paraffin, beeswax or soy wax.

- **Chunk** candles are decorative candles that are created by adding chunks of different colored waxes or other items to the hot wax so they become suspended in the candle as it hardens, or by embellishing the outside surface of the candle. There aren't any hard and fast rules to making these candles, as long as you don't include substances that might interfere with how they burn. You can also purchase decorative molds that will give your candles a sculpted look.

- **Container** candles are a favorite for beginning candle makers because you don't need to worry about releasing them from a mold or about what kind of wax to use. Since these candles don't have to support themselves, they can be made with palm, soy, beeswax, paraffin, paraffin/soy mixtures, and even gel. Clear containers such as glass jars are ideal for candles that contain decorative elements, or for gel candles where you want to emphasize the translucency and color of the gel, but you can also use other containers, such as tin cans.

CANDLE WAXES

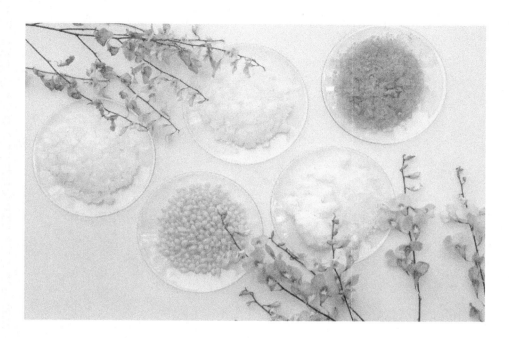

While medieval chandlers were limited to tallow, and hobbyists a few decades ago could basically choose between paraffin and beeswax, there are several additional candle making materials available today. Here are the basics about the unique qualities, functionalities, and drawbacks of the most common candle waxes.

Paraffin

Paraffin is essentially the default candle wax. The utility candles you can buy in the supermarket are all made out of paraffin, as are most of the fancy candles you see in gift shops. Paraffin is relatively inexpensive and very versatile. It's available in a range of melting points, making it suitable for almost all candle types, and it mixes easily with color dyes, fragrances and essential oils. It's a great choice for the beginning candle maker because it's easy to work with and inexpensive to experiment with. More advanced hobbyists appreciate it for its strength—even tall, skinny taper candles won't bend or break if they're made of paraffin—and for the fact that it never becomes frosted.

If there's a downside to paraffin, it's that it's refined from crude oil—yes, just like gasoline. That's not ideal from an environmental standpoint, so you might want to avoid paraffin if sustainability is a priority for you. You should also avoid it if you have asthma, as the hydrocarbons it releases when it burns produce a faint chemical odor that can cause breathing difficulties in sensitive individuals. Some paraffin candles have also been found to release cancer-causing ketones.

Soy

Soy wax was developed about 30 years ago and is currently the second most popular candle wax. Made from soybean oil, it's an all-natural wax which is almost as versatile as paraffin and much less expensive than beeswax. Soy is significantly softer than paraffin, though, so it's not the best choice for tapers or tall pillars. As like paraffin, it usually comes either in flakes or in blocks.

Pure soy wax can also be a little hard to find. Soy/paraffin blends are quite common, and a wax can claim to be "soy-based" if it contains at least 51% soy wax. If using soy is important to you for environmental or health reasons, take the time to read the label before you make your purchase. On the other hand, if you want something a little more natural than pure paraffin and a little more durable than pure soy, a blend like this may be exactly what you're looking for.

Palm wax is another plant-based option, and palm wax candles have a nice glow that makes them an excellent choice for use in home decor if beeswax isn't in the budget.

Beeswax

Beeswax is the most traditional and most treasured candle wax of all. It's completely natural and has a pleasantly sweet but mild scent and a truly beautiful internal glow. There's nothing more enchanting than the glow of a beeswax candle on a moonlit night. Like other waxes, beeswax is available as blocks and chips that can be melted and poured into molds; uniquely, it also comes as sheets that can simply be rolled to into tapers or pillars with nothing more than a wick and a few minutes of your time.

Of course, a wax as elegant and luxurious as beeswax doesn't come cheap. But as a bonus, beeswax has other applications—it can be used in many homemade beauty products, for instance. And beeswax candles double as air purifiers because they emit negative ions that fight airborne viruses and bacteria.

Gel

One of the most popular candle waxes isn't really a wax at all. Gel "wax" is a soft, translucent substance made from a combination of mineral oil and resins. It's usually sold clear and unscented so you can add your own colors and fragrances, but pre-colored types are available as well.

Because it's so soft, gel wax isn't well suited for pillars and tapers. It's usually used in glass container candles, often with decorative objects like seashells, little toys, or flower petals suspended inside. With a big enough container, you can even create an entire themed scene in your gel candle!

The best things about gel candles are their amazing looks and beautiful glow, but they have a couple of other advantages over wax candles as well. They don't make a mess, and they usually last longer because the gel melts completely when you burn them. When it cools after you snuff out the flame, the candle will take the shape of the jar again within a few hours. It's almost like having a brand new candle! Furthermore, because you don't need a double boiler and you don't have to pour them, gel candles also require less time and equipment than wax ones. So don't be afraid to give them a try—after which you can give them as amazing gifts!

PERSONALIZING YOUR CANDLES WITH COLOR DYES AND FRAGRANCES

Dyes

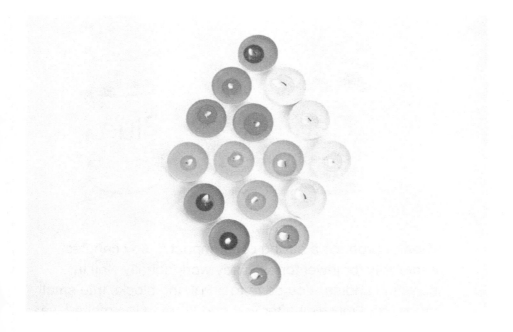

There are colored candle waxes available, but most of the wax used in homemade candles are sold in its pure, undyed form. White wax provides you with a blank canvas for your candle creations. The only questions are what colors to choose—and how to go about adding those colors to your wax.

Candle dyes come in the form of chips or flakes, blocks, and liquid, with each type having its own color effects. But it's not just the type of dye that determines the final color of your candles: The type of wax is also important. With soy wax, even dark colors will come out lighter than you'd expect. With paraffin wax, the color usually doesn't change all that much.

- **Liquid dyes** produce lighter shades in soy wax and slightly darker shades in paraffin.

- **Blocks** produce a strong color impact in soy candles, especially for jewel tones. They work equally well in paraffin candles. You have to break the blocks into small pieces and mix well after you add them to the melted wax.

- **Chips/flakes** are the easiest to use and provide the subtlest colors. In soy wax, this means soft, light pastel shades. When used in paraffin wax, dye chips produce slightly darker hues, although the colors are still light to medium at most.

With reasonably priced candle dyes readily available online and in craft stores, there's really no reason to use anything else to color your candles. And there are some things you definitely *shouldn't* use—specifically, food coloring and crayons. These are chemically incompatible with candle wax and can interfere with proper wicking. Dyes are one area where you don't want to get too creative with your candle making.

Except when it comes to colors! If you already have some creative inspiration going on, then by all means, go with it. But if you're anything like me, the blank canvas of pure wax will leave you with so many ideas that you won't know where to start.

Having a theme in mind or creating candles to match a specific decor is a good place to start. It's also worth considering the emotions and symbolism associated with various colors. Here is a quick guide to color energy and symbolism to help you choose the perfect hues for your creations.

- **White:** This perfectly neutral color blends in well with most decors. Depending on the type of wax used, your candles can range anywhere from a pristine white to a soft cream. White candles lend an atmosphere of serenity and calmness to any room. From a spiritual standpoint, white candles are often used in religious/spiritual ceremonies, and they're thought to have protective qualities.

- **Blue:** Next to white, blue is one of the most relaxing colors you can use in your candle creations. The range of hues runs from the softest blue pastel to brilliant, bold jewel tones. The color blue brings peace and tranquility, along with balance and healing.

- **Purple/Indigo:** Hues in this range are often thought of as being connected with all things on a spiritual level. They're thus useful for meditation, connecting with one's spiritual side, and simply as a color that brings many blessings. Purple is also a great color for creativity and works well in spaces where creative energy flows.

- **Pink:** Pink is the color of love, romance, and soft innocence. Pink candles are the perfect complements to rooms where you want to infuse a loving, peaceful atmosphere. Pink is a good color for candlelit family dinners or as a gift for someone with a special place in your heart.

- **Green:** Green is the color of grounding and stability. Candles of this color are a good choice when someone is feeling a little "flighty" or unsure of their future. Green is also the color of prosperity and growth, making candles of this color the perfect gift for someone starting a new adventure—such as a housewarming gift for a new homeowner or a present for someone who has just started a new job.

- **Yellow:** Yellow is the color of sunlight and positivity. Yellow candles are perfect for rooms where energy or creativity is important. Try a yellow candle—maybe scented with a bright, invigorating citrus scent—in a home office or on a table in a breakfast nook where you spend part of your morning.

- **Red:** Red, along with shades of orange, represents strong energy. Red is the color of passion, movement, and strength. Of course, red candles are well suited as decor for various holidays, but they can be used any time of year to add a positive, high-energy vibe to any room. Red is also considered the color of vitality and health, making a red candle a great gift for someone who's recovering from an illness or injury.

- **Black:** Formerly disfavored, black has become more of a neutral color that works well even with minimalist decors. From an energy standpoint, black signifies endings, cleansing and an opportunity to start anew. Bear in mind that you need a really high-quality dye to achieve a deep, intense black color in your candles.

Fragrances

Fragrance Oils

The most common method of adding scent to homemade candles is the use of synthetic fragrance oils, which are relatively inexpensive and available in an incredibly vast range of scents. Do a quick search on the internet and you'll find that there's no shortage of fragrance oil suppliers. They'll all have basic scents in stock—florals, fruits, etc.—and some offer more complex blends and even formulas that replicate designer fragrances. Start with a few of your favorites and you'll soon amass a collection of different fragrances that you can use individually or mix to create your own signature scents.

Quality counts when buying fragrances. Inferior grades won't smell quite right, and they may contain toxins or irritants that can trigger breathing difficulties. Always buy fragrance oils from reputable manufacturers. If you happen to live near a craft or hobby store that carries candle scents, it's worth the trip to smell a few in person before buying any online. However, that's not foolproof: Because fragrance oils are concentrated, it can be difficult to get a good feel for how the finished product will smell. So do your research and pay attention to consumer reviews to get the most authentic and consistent scents for your money.

Essential Oils

There are different schools of thought on whether you should use essential oils to add fragrance to your candles. Here, I'll present both sides of the argument, along with a few tips for best practices should you choose to use them.

When you burn a candle in your home, you're also releasing combustion byproducts of everything that is contained within the wax and wick. Because your home is an enclosed space, it's wise to choose your wax, wick and other additives carefully to ensure that you're minimizing exposure to unnecessary toxins. The threat of particulate matter being released into the air is why the U.S. Consumer Product Safety Commission (CPSC) banned the manufacture, importation, or selling of candles with lead wicks in 2003.

Those who focus on clean living may also be concerned about the chemicals used in synthetic candle fragrances. Because these fragrances come from a wide variety of manufactures, it's difficult (if not impossible) to know for sure what's in that little bottle—and what airborne toxins you might be exposing yourself, your family and your pets to.

Those worries vanish when you're using essential oils, at least if you're using pure, high-quality ones. Essential oils are the oils extracted from various parts of plants. The most reputable manufacturers sell oils that are 100% pure, with no additives whatsoever. However, cheaper essential oils are often of lesser quality oils and may be cut with additional unknown substances.

The theory behind using essential oils in candles is that you're minimizing exposure to toxic chemicals, and maybe even providing a few health benefits, while releasing a pleasant scent throughout the area. Sounds great—so what's the downside?

The problem with pure essential oils is that they're designed for therapeutic use, not as fragrances. Because of this, their scent isn't as concentrated as synthetic fragrance oils, and you may have to use quite a lot of essential oil to produce the desired effect. Using too much essential oil can affect the appearance of your candles, making them mottled or sweaty. Furthermore, some candle making enthusiasts say that even with a relatively large quantity of essential oil, scent output is minimal or distorted from what the pure oil puts off on its own.

Something else to keep in mind is that essential oils aren't intended to be used as perfumes. Each oil has therapeutic properties and contains volatile compounds. What might seem like a harmless fragrance additive can produce an undesired reaction, especially in children, pets, or individuals with allergies, compromised immune systems, or otherwise sensitive health.

If you choose to use essential oils in your candles, be aware that you'll need to use them differently than you would use traditional fragrance oils. Also, keep in mind where the candles will be burned, and don't use essential oils that may cause an adverse reaction in sensitive individuals. If you plan on gifting or selling your candles, stick to essential oils that are generally well tolerated by most people—like lavender, chamomile or geranium.

Here are a few additional points to keep in mind when using essential oils in your candle making.

- Essential oils are volatile and fragile, so take care to store them properly. As a general rule of thumb, store essential oils in a cool, dry place that's away from direct sunlight and open flame. Keep them in dark colored glass bottles instead of plastic.

- Placing drops of essential oil near the wick of a candle is not advised. If you want the scent from an essential oil, but don't want to use it in your candle making, rub a little of the oil on the outside of the candle. The gentle heat coming from the candle will help disperse the scent.

- Don't assume that because essential oils are natural they're all gentle. Some oils, like cinnamon and clove, are actually caustic when applied directly to the skin without being diluted in a carrier oil. If you're using any essential oil in your candle making, it's smart to wear a pair of gloves to prevent possible skin irritation.

- Only purchase essential oils from reputable retailers and manufacturers. There's a reason why there is such a vast difference in the price of essential oils among brands, and in this case, you almost always get what you pay for. Less expensive, inferior oils may be cut with added ingredients that you don't want in your candles or floating through the air in your home.

ESSENTIAL TOOLS OF
THE TRADE

Every candle maker needs a toolkit. Just how expansive that toolkit is will be entirely up to you. If you like a rustic look to your candles, you'll be able to get by with purchasing just a few materials and then filling in the gaps with items you have around your home. If you're after a high-end, professional look, you're going to want to invest a little more in items like molds, additives and releasing agents that improve the final appearance of your candles and increase their lifespan.

While you're probably excited about starting your candle making adventures, you should ease your way into the process. There's no point in buying all the bells and whistles until you know for certain that candle making is an art that you truly enjoy—which it will no doubt eventually become.

This section describes some of the basic tools of the trade— aside from wax—that you need for successful candle making. As you become more comfortable with your candle making abilities, you can add more candle making supplies. Let's dig in and look at the basics that you'll need to get started.

Wicks

Every candle needs a wick, but does it really matter what type or size of wick you use? The answer is yes, absolutely. The performance of a candle is largely determined by the wick. Using the wrong wick can cause your candles to burn improperly and shorten their lifespan. Proper wick selection makes the candle more reliable and longer lasting. Unfortunately, choosing the right wick can be a little confusing. The first time you go into the candle making supply section of your local craft store, you may feel completely overwhelmed by all the wick options. There are many different wick materials available, and they all come in different sizes, too. So in this section, we'll explain all about what they are and how to pick the best one for your candle.

A burning wick melts the surrounding wax and draws it in and up towards the flame, where it is used as fuel. In scented candles, the wick also helps to vaporize and disperse the fragrance. How a candle burns depends on both the wick and the wax. However, it is the wick that controls the temperature. The lower the temperature, the slower the wick will burn and the slower the wax will melt. Thus, you need to choose a wick that will burn at the right temperature for your candle.

When it comes to determining burn temperature, the size of the wick is much more important than the material it's made of. (Note that "size" here refers to thickness; any wick can easily be trimmed to fit the length of your candle.) Using a wick of the wrong size will almost always result in inefficient combustion, wax pooling, and/or excessive smoke output. If the wick is too small, the wax will melt but the wick will eventually fall over and go out. If the wick is too large, it will vaporize the candle before you know it. A correctly sized wick will keep the candle glowing longer and vaporizes the wax cleanly without creating much smoke.

So how do you figure out the correct wick size for a particular candle? Factors to consider include the diameter of the candle, the type of wax, the burn rate of the wick, the melting point of the wick coating, and any fragrance or color additives you're using. You'll get more of a feel for this as you make more candles, but no matter how experienced you become, wick sizing will likely remain one of your biggest challenges. It's never going to be a good idea to rely solely on your intuition—and fortunately, you don't have to. Wick manufacturers test their products thoroughly and include comprehensive specifications and suggestions on the packaging. Always consult this information in order to choose a wick that's perfectly paired with your candle.

The type of wick to use also depends on things like the type of wax you're using, the size and shape of your candle, and fragrance/color additives. Once again, you should refer to the manufacturer's guidelines for best results, but here's a quick look at different wick types to get you started:

- **Cored** wicks are made from braided or knitted fiber and contain a rigid core material that makes them self-supporting and structurally stable. Common core materials include zinc, cotton, and paper. Zinc is the most popular and the most rigid; it won't leak or break even at high temperatures. Cotton core wicks are the most flexible. Cored wicks can be used in most candles, but they're absolutely essential in projects that require a self-supporting wick, such as votives, novelty candles, and some pillars.

- **Flat** wicks are made from braided fiber and are less rigid than cored wicks. They are the best choice for long candles such as tapers and pillars because they are durable and burn consistently over time. Flat wicks will bend and "self-trim" while burning, which prevents carbon from building up at the tip of the wick and creating a mushroom effect.

- **Square braid** wicks are structurally similar to flat wicks, but they're braided in a way that makes them slightly more rounded or square. Like flat wicks, square braids bend slightly when lit and will self-trim. The main difference is that square braids are a little thicker and sturdier. That makes them more resistant to clogging, which means they're the best option for beeswax candles and for any candles with a lot of fragrance and color additives that would clog up a less robust wick structure.

There are also a variety of specialty wicks that you might want to explore for certain candle making projects.

- **CD** wicks have a paper core designed specifically for paraffin, soy wax and gel candles, which burn light and slow. They're good in container candles and votives but are unsuitable for scented candles.

- **CDN** wicks are for use only with paraffin wax. They're mostly used in pillar candles, but can also be good for solid color container candles.

- **HTP** (high-tension paper) wicks contain a paper core that has been woven into the surrounding fibers. This provides more stability than the standard paper core wick, so HTP wicks are a good choice for container candles, including votives.

- **LX** wicks are flat, braided wicks with special threads that provide additional stabilization. They are durable and burn steadily, making them suitable for tall pillar and container candles, and can be used with a variety of waxes.

- **Ply cotton** wicks, like CDN wicks, are compatible only with paraffin wax. They work well in taper and pillar candles.

- **RRD** wicks are round wicks that contain a cotton core with specially woven tension threads. This type of wick is and very versatile, making it a top choice for candle makers who work with a variety of waxes. It's also strong, so it's great for container candles and votives. Because of the tension, RRD wicks stand up well to fragrance and color additives.

- **Wooden** wicks are made out of thin, light pieces of wood. They are usually an inch wide and come in different lengths. Wooden wicks can be used with all kinds of wax, including beeswax, but they work best with paraffin and soy wax. They make a little crackling sound as they burn and are usually used in luxury candles intended for home decor. They're more expensive than ordinary fiber candle wicks, and you should buy the best ones you can find— they'll last a lot longer.

So, as you can see, there really isn't a one-size-fits-all solution to choosing wicks. If you're planning on making candles in a variety of styles, you're also going to need a variety of wicks. Some companies will even make custom wicks upon request. This can come in handy once you have a lot of experience in candle making and are able to explain your requirements in detail. But standard wicks should be all you need for making most candles.

As with any product, wicks vary in quality. Some will burn cleanly while others will display unsightly carbon buildup even if you've done everything right. Do some research to find a good brand, and look for wicks that seem sturdy and well-formed. One way to assess the quality of a wick is by looking at what it does when you extinguish the candle. A good wick will glow for some time after the flame disappears. When you see that afterglow, you can feel confident about buying more wicks from the same supplier.

Molds and Containers

Unless you're making tapers or rolled candles, you're going to need either a mold or some type of container. From a budget standpoint, this is one of the most versatile areas of candle making: You can buy professional quality molds and fancy containers, or you can repurpose items you already have around your house.

Store-bought candle molds will usually give you a more consistent shape, a smoother finish, and an easier release. They come in a wide range of shapes and sizes and may be made from plastic, metal or silicone. The premium option here is metal molds, which give your candles a smooth surface and a nice shape, work well with all kinds of wax, and will last forever as long as you use them carefully.

Plastic molds are cheaper, so they're a reasonable choice if you're just trying out candle making and don't want to spend a whole lot of money at first. They also come in a lot of fun shapes like orbs, pyramids, and other geometrical solids. You won't find such variety in metal molds.

On the other hand, if you want to use something of high quality, you won't like plastic molds much. They leave a scruffy surface on candles from the beginning, and they're also prone to scratches. Once they get scratched, your candles will come out scratchy too. That may be fine when you're a beginner, but once you can make candles proficiently and are looking for perfection, the best option would be metal molds. Furthermore, you can't really use plastic molds for scented candles. The inside of the mold gets ruined by the fragrance oils, and your candles will come out looking stained and rough.

Silicone molds have become very popular for candle making nowadays. These versatile molds aren't just for candles; you can make great soaps or cakes as well. They're highly flexible, so you can get many unique shapes out of them and really express your creativity. Doing so calls for some more advanced, professional-level candle making techniques, though, so it's better to master plastic and metal molds before moving on to silicone.

As you begin your candle making journey, I'd recommend purchasing a couple of molds—maybe a metal one and a plastic one—and then trying out a variety of homemade molds as well. This will give you an idea of the difference in the end products and allow you to get a feel for candle making without breaking the bank.

What items can you repurpose as candle making molds? Just about anything you can think of, as long as it can withstand the heat of the hot wax and allow for an easy release of the finished candle. A few examples of repurposed candle molds include:

- Aluminum or tin cans
- Milk cartons, both cardboard, and plastic
- Flower pots (these should be treated with a silicone sealant to prevent the wax from seeping into the mold)

- Silicone kitchen molds (such as ice cube molds, baking molds, and candy molds)
- Cups
- Paper towel rolls
- Small bowls
- Metal baking tins
- Basically, any hollow container you have around the house

The same idea holds true for containers. You can certainly purchase containers for your candles. Supermarkets sell standard jars for next to nothing, and craft stores will have a selection of different sizes and shapes available for not much more. However, chances are you already have lots of suitable containers around your home—mason jars or other glass jars, canisters, tin cans, pottery, glasses, or even seashells.

Just make sure the container is clean, dry, and can withstand the heat. Don't try to make container candles in any item that's even remotely flammable. For example, you could use a cardboard milk carton as a mold for a candle, but you wouldn't want to use it as a container to hold the candle while it's burning.

Other Essentials

Here are a few more essentials that you'll want to add to your candle making toolbox. Even if you already have some of these items around your house, you'll want a set that's dedicated to candle making. For example, you're probably not going to want to use your double boiler for anything else once it has been used for melting wax.

- Double boiler or warmer designed for melting wax
- Food grade thermometer
- Kitchen scale
- Dipping can (for tapers)
- Ladle (for pouring candles)
- Dowels or bamboo sticks (for supporting the wick while the candle is hardening)
- Wicking tool or wicking needle (for molded candles)
- Wick weights (for container candles)
- Rack to hang dipped candles
- Mold releasing agent
- Silicone sealant
- Cookie sheets or silicone mats to work on
- Oven mitts
- UV inhibitor (to prevent discoloration)
- Glue gun
- Baking paper

That's everything, and these supplies can be purchased from any local craft store at a reasonable cost. They'll pay for themselves with the first batch of candles you make. Now let's take a look at a few of them in more detail.

- A **double boiler** is the most convenient way to melt wax. You can improvise with a couple of pots, but it's easiest if you buy a double boiler. One part of the boiler gets filled with water, which is heated and in turn melts the wax. Never melt wax over direct heat—it will stick to your equipment and be difficult to clean up.

- You don't need **candle sealant** if you're making container candles, but it's great to have if you're using a mold. It helps prevent the wax from leaking from the base of the mold, which keeps the candle intact and the countertop clean. A good candle sealant will last for multiple candles.

- **Wick holders** keep the wicks in place while you pour the molten wax. If the wick ends up in the wrong place the candle won't burn properly, so wick holders are a necessity whether you're using a mold or a container. You can buy dowels or bamboo sticks for this purpose, or you can just use a pen or pencil instead. **Wick weights**, meanwhile, serve the same purpose at the bottom of container candles. Any small piece of metal that you can wrap the wick around should work fine, but you can also purchase wick weights.

- A **wicking needle** really helps when you're making mold candles. It allows you to take out the wick from the other side of the mold. If you have one, this process is hassle-free; if you don't it can be a nightmare to do it for the first time. Wicking needles come in different sizes for different sized molds, so make sure you get one that's appropriate for the hole in your mold. Or you can just get a set of needles in various sizes.

- You can use a **hot glue gun** to attach wicks to the bottom of container candles as an alternative to wick weights. But this tool doesn't just heat glue; it can also measure the temperature of molten candle wax when you're ready to pour it into the container. And having a hot glue gun will prove to be a great help for a lot of DIY projects. So invest a little in one of these gadgets—you'll get a lot of convenience in return.

49

All of these candle making supplies are helpful for preparing the best possible candles. But if you don't want to purchase them all right now, that's okay. You can get started with the basic equipment and materials and purchase additional items as you become more proficient and want to add more creativity to your homemade candles.

SAFETY

Candle making can be a messy process even for the most experienced crafters. You're dealing with hot wax or gel, which can cause severe burns, plus additives that aren't always forgiving if you happen to spill them. No matter how careful you are, accidents are bound to happen, so it's best to prepare for them.

So before you get elbow deep into the candle making process, take the time to prepare your space. You want a clear workspace with everything that you'll need within easy reach. You also need to protect flooring and furniture from the inevitable spills. If possible, avoid working over a carpeted area, but if this can't be done then consider purchasing mats for the area where you'll be working directly with hot wax.

You should also make sure you have a fire extinguisher and a first aid kit for burns within reach. This might seem extreme, but you'll most probably be making candles in your kitchen, and it's not a bad idea to have a fire extinguisher there anyway. Accidents happen when you're least expecting them, and this safety equipment can save you from bodily harm or costly damage to your home. Keep the fire extinguisher near you when you are making candles and use it immediately on any fire so that it does not spread.

Proper ventilation is an absolute must when making candles. When you light a candle, the wax melts and evaporates into the air *slowly*. When you're melting a larger quantity of wax over higher heat, much more of it finds its way into the air that you're breathing. Keeping your work area well ventilated will minimize the amount of wax particles building up in the air. And, of course, ventilation is especially important when working with concentrated fragrance additives, which can be irritating to the eyes, nose and throat when used in larger quantities.

Any wax which you are not using should not be near the flame. Even if it doesn't catch fire, it will be useless if it melts inside the bag, because the plastic from the bag will contaminate it. Keep the bag of color dye away from the heat as well, as this can leave stains on the countertop if it melts.

Never touch the pot in which you have melted the wax with your bare hands. It can burn you badly, so always handle it with a potholder or oven mitt.

Monitor the temperature of the wax continuously. If it overheats, it can burn. If you are using natural soy wax or paraffin wax without color dye, you may see a burned color when this happens, but in any event burnt wax doesn't make good candles. So keep checking the wax with a thermometer and shut off the flame when it reaches the desired temperature.

Always check the temperature before pouring the wax into a mold or container, too. Sometimes melted wax can be relatively cool, but other times it can be really hot. Pouring the candles is the trickiest part of the process and requires a lot of practice to get right. It helps if you start out by making smaller candles so you don't need to fill up the entire boiler with melted wax on your first few attempts. As you get used to it, you can melt larger quantities of wax. But no matter how experienced you are, always be careful and attentive when you are pouring the candles, and always wear gloves so that you won't get wax on your hands if there's a spill. If you have children, don't do any pouring while they're around.

Chances are that you're going to have at least a little bit of wax left over after pouring your last candle. It's better to prepare too much wax than not enough, but that leaves you with leftover wax that you'll need to do something with. First, never ever pour wax down the drain. Yes, this seems like common sense, but you'd be surprised how instinctive it is to pour something that comes from a double boiler down the drain without even thinking about it. This can cause major havoc for your plumbing system. What's less obvious is that you shouldn't even pour the water used in your double boiler down the drain. Often, little droplets of wax will find their way into this water, and again, this can damage plumbing if you're not careful.

Lighting your finished candle for the first time is always exciting, but safety is still important. Keep your house well ventilated when burning candles. Don't close the windows to concentrate the fragrance; keep them open so that the air can flow through the room where you have placed the candles. Burning candles in a closed-up house can make it hard to breathe, so adequate ventilation is essential.

In general, be careful whenever you have a candle lit—remember that it's a little fire inside your house. Don't light a candle near paper, leaves, or other materials that can catch fire easily. Put your candle somewhere safe and out of reach of children so that you can do your housework without worrying about it. Don't light a candle and then go to bed so that you can smell it as you drift off to sleep. If the candle is knocked over by a breeze or a cat, or if it melts completely with the wick still burning, you may never wake up! If you light a candle, then take responsibility for snuffing it out too.

But don't worry too much—simply be careful when you are making and burning your candles, and it will be a wonderful experience for you.

MAKING YOUR CANDLES STEP-BY-STEP

Congratulations, you've done the research, learned the basics of getting started with candle making, chosen your wax and additives, and have all your equipment at hand. You're officially ready to roll up your sleeves and get busy making some candles. All you need now is the step-by-step path to making your candle making visions a reality.

Before you begin any candle making project, it's a good idea to review the instructions and have a plan in place—even if it seems like you've already made a specific type of candle a hundred times before. It's easy to forget something or let an important detail slide. It's always better to take a few extra minutes to be prepared than to risk compromising your candle making due to an avoidable mistake.

Rolled Beeswax Candles

We'll start this section with rolled candles since they're the absolute easiest for beginners. Rolled candles are made from sheets of wax, usually beeswax because it's softer and more pliable. Tapers are the most popular form of rolled candles, although you could try your hand at making something a little thicker, like a pillar that's a couple of inches in diameter.

You can purchase sheets of wax from a craft store or online retailer. When you start shopping, you'll find that many sheets of wax are embossed to look like honeycombs. If you're not fond of this look, you can find plain, un-embossed sheets of beeswax, although it might take a little more digging.

Sheet wax is available in a variety of colors, but since it comes ready to roll, you won't be able to add any additional colorant dyes or fragrances. If you really want a scented candle, you can rub a little fragrance or essential oil on the outside of the candle before you light it.

Choose a wick that's suitable for tapers or pillars made from beeswax and that corresponds to the planned diameter of your candle. The manufacturer's guidelines will be able to assist you in picking the correct wick.

When trimming your wick, line it up lengthwise alongside the sheet of wax you'll be using. Your wick should be about 1½ to 2 inches longer than your candle.

You'll find it helpful to have a tool for gently warming the wax just enough to make it more pliable. Try a hair dryer or even an iron on very low heat (with a piece of wax paper separating the iron from the wax).

1. Prepare a clean work surface.

2. Lay out a sheet of wax.

3. Measure and cut your wick according to the length of your candle, leaving 1½ to 2 inches of extra wick.

4. If you're familiar enough with sheet wax that you can gauge the width based on the diameter of candle you want to make, you can trim the wax now. Otherwise, you can trim it after it has been rolled.

5. Gently warm the wax with a hair dryer to make it more pliable. Do not heat the wax to the point that it melts.

6. Working along a lengthwise edge, fold over a small strip of the wax, about ⅛ of an inch.

7. Place the wick inside the fold and line it up properly along the bottom.

8. Press the fold gently to secure the wick.

9. Begin to roll the wax—tightly but not so tightly that you risk breaking or tearing it. You'll be able to feel a good tension point.

10. As you roll the wax, make sure that the wick stays snug and secure in the center.

11. Once you've reached the desired diameter, use a sharp blade to make a smooth cut in the sheet of wax if it hasn't already been trimmed. (Many sheets of wax will already be perfectly sized for tapers.)

12. Gently press the trimmed edge into the candle to secure it. You shouldn't need to press it so hard that it indents, but you do want to make sure that it adheres to the candle. Use a hairdryer if needed to warm the wax to create a seal.

13. Trim the wick at the top of the candle, leaving about ½ inch for lighting.

14. Place the candle upright to make sure that it stands even. If the bottom surface isn't level, trim the bottom of the candle to create a flat surface. Again, you can use a hairdryer to smooth and flatten the bottom of your candle if necessary.

Molded Candles

Pillar candles are a little more complex than rolled candles, but with a little practice and patience, you'll be a pro in no time. The good news is that once you master the art of the pillar candle, other molded candles are a breeze—no matter how complex the shape or design. Here's how to do it:

1. If you're using block wax, break or cut it up into small pieces of uniform size. This will ensure that it melts evenly and the temperature remains consistent throughout the molten wax.

2. Coat the inside of the mold with a releasing agent, if necessary. You don't need to use a releasing agent every time you use a mold, as some residue will remain. Applying the releasing agent once every five pours or so should be sufficient to provide a smooth release.

3. Thread the wick into the mold with a wicking needle. Pass the needle through the base, leaving the wick behind. (Pushing the needle through the mold may require some pressure.) Leave several inches of wick protruding from the top of the mold.

4. Use candle sealant to plug the bottom of the mold. You can also put some candle sealant around the wick to help it stay in place.

5. Wrap the protruding part of the wick around a dowel, bamboo stick or pencil. Rest it on top of the mold so that the wick is straight and centered. This will help keep the wick in the right place when you are pouring the molten wax into the mold.

6. Place the wax in a double boiler and heat it while stirring gently. Once the water boils, turn down the heat and let it simmer. The wax should melt within a few minutes. It's ready once it turns transparent and reaches about 200°F on the thermometer.

7. If you're making colored candles, now's the time to add the dye. Before the wax cools below 190°F, add 1–1½ tablespoons of dye. Stir vigorously and make sure that the dye mixes well. The dye needs to be completely dissolved, and if that is not happening you may have to return the wax to the boiler and heat it up again. The color will lighten somewhat as the wax cools down. So the question is, how much dye do you need to add to get the candle color you want? One quick way to predict the final color is to pour a little wax onto some baking paper. As soon as it hardens, you'll know the actual color of the completed candle. Any droplets of wax that have dried on the bowl will also be a good guide. Evaluate the color quickly—you don't have a lot of time before the wax cools too much to add more dye—and then add another 1–1½ tablespoons of dye if needed.

8. Let the wax cool to the optimal pouring temperature. This will vary depending on the type of wax you're using, so refer to the manufacturer's instructions. As a general rule, soy wax should be poured between 120°F and 140°F, and paraffin is best poured between 180°F and 190°F. When the wax is poured at the correct temperature, the candle will be free from bubbles and have a perfect finish.

9. Meanwhile, preheat your mold. The mold doesn't need to be hot by any means, but some molds, especially metal ones, may be too cold at room temperature. Warming your mold is another way to get smooth candles with a perfectly lustrous finish.

10. Once the wax has cooled to pouring temperature, add any fragrance oil right before pouring.

11. Carefully pour the wax into the mold, making sure that the wick remains straight. The wax will settle some as it cools, so you should leave a bit of room—an inch or so—to accommodate a second pour after the wax begins to cool.

12. Let the candle set for an hour or two. The wax should still be slightly warm to the touch but beginning to firm up.

13. Use a bamboo stick to make a few holes in the candle, all the way down to the bottom of the mold. The holes should be near the wick, but make sure that you don't accidentally disturb it. These holes will open up any voids inside the candle and let the wax cool down faster.

14. Top off the candle with some more molten wax. Avoid pouring the wax directly over the wick.

15. Let the candle set until completely cooled and hardened. The size of your candle will determine how long this takes, but it's better to err on the side of caution. Removing it too soon can affect the appearance of your candle and compromise its structural integrity.

16. As long as the wax has cooled completely, getting it out of the mold shouldn't be a hassle. However, if you're having a hard time, just put it in the fridge for 20 minutes or so and then you will be able to pull it out smoothly.
17. Trim the wick (on both sides) and light it to see the candle you made by yourself burn!

Isn't it amazing? All that beauty from a quick, easy process! Doing it just once will teach you all about it, and you can go on to make thousands of other candles with different colors and fragrances in them.

Container Candles

The process for making container candles is very similar to that of making molded candles. You can basically follow the instructions above with a just a few modifications.

First, while you won't have to worry about threading the wick into a mold, you still need to keep it steady. You can handle this the same way at the top of the container, by wrapping the excess wick around a dowel or bamboo stick. At the bottom, you'll have to attach it to a wick weight or stick it to the container using a hot glue gun to keep it from floating away.

Second, if you're using gel wax, which is best suited for container candles, make sure that you've read the instructions carefully. This type of wax needs to be handled a little differently than paraffin or beeswax. You don't use a double boiler; instead, you add the candle gel directly to the container and put it into the oven. The oven should be set to 225°F. The gel will melt slowly—it takes more time than melting the wax for wax candles—so you'll have to be patient. Once it does melt, stir the gel gently, slowly, and thoroughly to remove any bubbles, making sure not to disturb the wick as you do. If you want to embed any decorative items in the gel, you can do that next.

Since the purpose of container candles is usually to add a nice decorative touch, you might want to experiment with using different colored waxes. If you choose to use different colored waxes within one candle, heat the wax to the optimal melting point, then carefully pour portions into tin cans where individual colors can be added. It's best if you can keep these cans warm; at the very least, you should warm them before you add the wax and dye to prevent the wax from cooling too quickly. Wait about half an hour after you pour the first color into your container before pouring the second layer on top of it; repeat for any additional layers.

To get an even consistency throughout your container candle, wait for the top of the candle to congeal slightly after you pour the wax. Use a toothpick or other sharp tool to poke a few holes in the skinned surface of the candle, then carefully top it off with warm wax. You may have to do a second pour if the wax settles too much, but this extra step will help fill in air gaps and ensure even consistency.

Here is a series of images showing the different steps for a container candle using paraffin wax and colored wax to make a striped candle. Wait approximatively 30 minutes between colors.

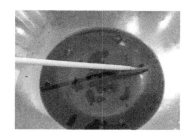

Fragrance Oils

If you would like to use fragrance oil in your container candles, after the wax has melted and reaches a temperature of 185°F, mix-in your chosen fragrance and stir well with wooden stick or spoon. The amount to use a general rule of thumb is 1 ounce per pound of wax. It's a good idea to weigh your fragrance oil rather than measure it for more precise measurement. Always cover your container with a lid to preserve the scent. Best is to let the candles cure for at least 3 days and optimally 10 days. Stove in a dry place away from excessive heat and light.

Dipped Candles

Here we come to the true labor of love in candle making—the dipped candle. Making dipped candles is a little more "hands-on" than making other types of candles. By this, I mean that it requires more than pouring, waiting to do a repour and then heading off to do something else. Dipped candles require your constant attention.

To make dipped tapers, you'll need:

- A double boiler that's deep enough to dip the entire length of the taper candle
- Long lengths of wick
- Wick weights
- A rod or other type of drying rack to hang your candles over as they set

The beginning stages of making dipped candles look very much like the steps for other types of candles.

1. Begin by preparing your work station, including setting up the rod or drying rack for your finished candles.

2. When preparing your wicks, keep in mind that each end of the wick is going to have a candle on it. It's necessary to dip candles this way so that each side will be evenly weighted as you hang them up to dry. You can't place dipped candles on a flat surface to harden them, because then one side of the candle would be flat rather than perfectly (or imperfectly) round.

3.   Say you're planning on making dipped candles that are about 6 inches long. You'll need to have 6 inches of wick for the candles at each end, plus a couple of inches for lighting. You'll also want to leave adequate space between the candles so that they can hang properly. To make two 6-inch dipped candles, you should count on anywhere from about 18–24 inches of wick.

4.   Attach a small wick weight at each end of the wick to help keep the wicks straight and secured in the middle of the candle.

5.   The canister that you melt your wax in needs to be deep enough to submerge the entire candle as you coat the wick. This means that you're going to need to melt significantly more wax than you'll actually need for the candles.

6.   Once the wax is heated and cooled slightly to the proper temperature, prime the wick by dipping it in the wax and then smoothing it out and making it straight. This step is important because a primed wick forms the skeleton of your dipped candle.

7.   Let the wax on the primed wick set until firm.

8.   Fold the wick in half so that both sides are the same length.

9.   Hold the wick so that the two sides dangle evenly with a couple of inches of space between them. It's best to string the wick over a tool, such as a piece of firm wire or a dowel, because it's more comfortable. Your hands might get tired of holding the candles while waiting for the wax to set between dips.

10. Slowly lower the wick ends into the warm wax up to the point that matches the candle length you're after.

11. Remove the wicks from the wax and allow the wax to set for a couple of minutes.

12. Dip the ends unto the wax again, allowing a second coat to build up over the first. Remove the wicks from the wax and allow them set for couple of minutes.

13. Continue repeating this process until the wax has built up to your desired thickness. Keep in mind how you'll be using your candles when determining how thick they should be. For instance, if you'll be using traditional taper holders, you'll want a width that fits snuggly in the holder. If your candles end up a little too thick, they can always be trimmed slightly to fit.

14. Once you've got a good coating of wax on the wicks, to the point that the wick is securely in place through the middle of the candle, you can cut off the wick weights. You don't want to wait too long to do this, because you might affect the final appearance of the candle.

15. Once you've dipped the candles to a satisfactory size, carefully hang the wicks over the rod or drying rack. Let them set several hours, or preferably overnight, before using. They can also be polished with a soft cloth once completely dry.

16. Take the candles off the rack and then trim the wicks, leaving about ½ inch for lighting on each candle.

Crayon Candles

As noted above, you shouldn't mix crayons into your wax candles because crayon wax isn't compatible with candle wax. But if you have enough old crayons lying around, you can make some great candles using nothing else. Here's how to do it.

1.   Choose the color combination you want to use. This is a crucial step, because mixing up all the colors randomly will be something of a disaster. You can probably figure out some basic combinations—red + yellow = orange etc.—on your own, and you can look online for additional inspiration.

2.   Unwrap all the crayons you're going to use. If you can't take the wrappers off easily, put them in a bowl with some cold water and ice cubes. Let them sit for about 10 minutes and you should be able to peel the wrappers off easily. You can also slit them with a knife and then slide them off.

3.   Put the crayons in a bowl and melt them in the microwave. For 12–15 crayons, this should take about two minutes. Check every 30 seconds to see if they are melting and stir gently. You can take them out once they're completely melted.

4.   Pour the melted crayons into a small mold or jar. Let the wax set for two hours. It will harden in less than two hours, but giving it this much time will provide you the best quality candles in the end.

5. So far, so easy, right? Well, now we come to the hardest part of making crayon candles—the choice of wick. The flat, braided LX wick is your best bet for crayon candles as it sticks well to crayon wax and can be used in any kind of container or mold. It's also very stable and won't move out of place. The next thing is to choose the right wick size. When you're using small containers or molds—as you usually are for crayon candles—then you have to be extra-careful that the wick is not too big. If it is, it will produce excessive smoke and cause the candle to burn too quickly. A candle that should last 5–6 hours may last only an hour if the wick is too large.

6. Now that you've selected an appropriate wick, you have to insert it into the candle. If you made the candle in a mold, remove it from the mold now. Next, use a bamboo stick or toothpick to punch a hole for the wick. Make sure it's the right size to accept the flat, braided wick, and don't go deeper than ½ inch above the base of the candle. (If the hole is punched completely through, the wick won't stay in place.) Insert the wick into the hole and press the wax together to hold it firmly.

Despite their humble origins, crayon candles can provide colorful beauty at any event. Why not try placing them on an aluminum tray decorated with roses? You'll love the look, and you won't be able to get over the fat that you have made it yourself!

TROUBLESHOOTING

The first lighting of a candle you've crafted yourself is a very rewarding experience. In an ideal world, each candle that you created would light perfectly, burn smoothly and maintain its beautiful appearance and scent as it burns.

In reality, a candle that burns perfectly while maintaining its functionality and aesthetic appeal isn't always the end result of your efforts. Mistakes happen, even for those who are experienced in the art of candle making. Fortunately, most problems that arise with candle making are relatively simple to troubleshoot and prevent in the future.

Here are a few of the most common problems that arise with home candle making, along with solutions that will get you back on track and have you creating gorgeous, perfectly functional candles in no time.

Cracks

Unless the candle was dropped or handled roughly, cracks, either on the surface or deeper into the body of the candle, are typically the result of a drastic change in temperature. For example, placing a freshly poured candle mold in the refrigerator or freezer to expedite the hardening process can cause the wax to become brittle and create cracks both small and large throughout the candle. Pouring hot wax into a mold to fill wells and voids after the candle has already hardened can also create cracks due to the temperature difference between the first and second pour of wax.

The best remedy for cracked candles is to avoid the situation by allowing your candles to cool and harden properly. Just let your candles set at the room temperature in which they were poured, away from any direct drafts, preferably on a cooling rack that allows the wax to solidify from the bottom up.

If a second pour is required, make sure that it's done while the wax in the mold is still somewhat warm and hasn't had the chance to harden completely.

Mottled Appearance

There are several factors that can lead to candles having a mottled, or splotchy, appearance. Improper cooling technique is one leading cause; another is the use of too much fragrance oil. Make sure that you're using the correct amount of fragrance oil in proportion to the amount of wax used.

If you're using the proper amount of fragrance oil and still experiencing this issue, it might be that there is an incompatibility between the type of wax and the fragrance additive that you're using, although this scenario is uncommon.

A mottled appearance can also be caused by forcing the release of your candles from their molds before they're fully set. This is most likely to happen with larger candles, such as tall pillars, since it's a little more difficult to gauge when these are completely set and hardened.

White, Powdery Appearance

What you're seeing is something called "bloom"—a term you might already be familiar with if you're a chocolate lover who has witnessed the same phenomenon on your chocolate bars. Although the causes are different, the result of a lightly powdery looking surface is similar.

There are several things that can affect the surface appearance of your candles, but bloom is usually confined to vegetable-based waxes, like soy. Bloom happens as the vegetable-based wax hardens and returns to its natural state.

In some mild cases, you might be able to buff the candle and soften the appearance of the bloom. Alternatively, you can just embrace it as giving your candles a unique character that doesn't affect their functionality whatsoever.

You can reduce the chances of bloom forming on your soy candles by pouring and setting your candles in a relatively warm room and allowing adequate space for them to "breathe" while hardening.

Soy Candles Change Colors

White or ivory soy candles are beautiful in their simplicity and make the perfect accompaniment to any decor. The only problem is that, over time, uncolored soy candles can take on a bit of a yellowish hue.

This is because soy wax is more sensitive to direct sunlight than other types of wax used in candle making. Exposure to UV rays can cause the wax to turn yellow, and in some cases, to appear dirty.

There are UV blockers that you can add to your soy candles if this is a problem for you, or if you're selling your candles and want them to stay pristine-looking long term to keep your customers happy. For personal use, you can also just keep soy candles out of direct sunlight to minimize discoloration.

Faded Candles

It's normal for colored candles to fade over time, especially if they're used primarily for decor purposes and exposed to sunlight throughout the day. So it's not just soy candles you should keep away from the sun—all type of candles that contain color additives can also be affected by direct sunlight.

If your candles are fading while stored in a cupboard or closet, it might be that the color additives you're using are of inferior quality. Shop around and choose the highest quality color additives that fit your budget.

Bubbles in the Wax

If your candles appear to have bubbles, either large or small, throughout the wax, chances are that it has something to do with how the wax was handled prior to pouring. Anything that adds bubbles into the wax while it's being heated has the potential to create little pockets of air in your candles. For example, stirring the wax too aggressively while heating it in an attempt to make it melt faster could cause bubbles.

Being impatient and pouring the wax too early can also cause little bubbles in your candles. It's perfectly normal for some air bubbles to be present when you pour candles. However, if your wax hasn't been heated to the proper temperature, it can cool too quickly. When this happens, the little air bubbles don't have time to rise to the surface and pop. Instead, they get trapped inside.

If you notice large bubbles forming around the top after your second pour, make sure that the wax from your first pour is still warm but slightly firm.

Air Bubbles in Glass Containers

It's very disappointing when your glass container candle looks like it has air bubbles along the sides. There are few things worse in the world of candle making than putting in the time and effort to create a perfect candle, only to have a minor aesthetic flaw take something away from all your hard work. Air bubbles, or "wet spots", in glass container candles are an issue that can affect a candle's visual appeal.

Air bubbles or wet spots can be seen in glass container candles where it looks like the wax has pulled away from the surface of the container in spots. This is a fairly common occurrence that you can often find even in high-end commercially produced candles.

Once one of these spots appears in a container candle, it can't be remedied. Fortunately, it doesn't affect the functionality of the candle in any way. Most of the time, these pockets are relatively small and don't present as a major flaw. Still, knowing how to avoid them will allow you to create glass container candles with smooth, flawless finish.

Wax can expand and contract due to temperature changes. In container candles, this causes the wax to pull away from the container surface, resulting in the visual bubble or area that looks like a wet spot. One of the most effective ways to avoid this is by providing a temperature-stable cooling environment. For instance, make sure your cooling rack isn't placed near an open window or drafty area in your home. If your candles are exposed to drafts, try placing a simple covering—such as a cardboard box—over them to reduce exposure to drafts and changes in temperature.

The condition of the containers is also important. Dirt, dust or moisture can cause the wax to pull away from the side, so make sure your containers are clean and dry. It's also a good idea to warm your containers slightly before pouring the hot wax into them. This can prevent the wax from expanding and contracting due to the temperature change.

"Sinkholes"

By sinkholes, we're referring to areas of the candle that seem to have sunken in. A candle that has caved in is not only unattractive but also more likely to burn inefficiently and have a reduced overall burn time. These areas might be small, but they can also cover a significant portion of your candle.

Sinkholes can be prevented with a little temperature control. It's important that your candles cool slowly, from the bottom up. An environment that is too cool can cause sinkholes, but often the cause is pouring wax before it has been heated to the proper point. This not only causes the wax to cool too quickly, but also to cool from the top down, which causes structural weaknesses in the candle.

Wax Pools

When wax pools around the center of the candle, it drowns the wick, eventually extinguishing the flame. After a while, the wick becomes saturated and completely submerged, leaving you making futile attempts at salvaging it. This is caused by a small or inadequate wax pool. Ideally, you want the wax pool to extend outward, covering a large percentage of the top of the candle. This ensures that the wick will function properly and that your candle will last as long as it's supposed to.

If wax pooling around your wick is problem, the solution lies in using the right sized wick—in this case, a larger one. Use the manufacturer's guidelines to determine the right size wick for the diameter of your candle. Larger candles may require more than one wick to burn properly.

If you've adjusted your wick size and are still experiencing issues with your wax pool, it could be that you've used too much fragrance or included additives that are incompatible with your candle wax.

"Sweaty" Candles

A "sweaty" residue may look like condensation forming on the outside of the candle, or you may see small beads of an oily-looking substance appearing on the wax. Most of the time this is the result of too much fragrance oil being used in the candle. Although it is less common, a candle may also appear to sweat if it is left in direct sunlight or exposed to excessive heat.

Soy wax is more prone to sweating than other types of candle wax, especially when fragrance oils are used. As a side note, sweating is mainly an aesthetic issue that won't affect the functionality of your candles.

Excessive Smoke

If your candle is putting off a small, barely noticeable amount of smoke, it really isn't a big deal—after all, you *are* burning something! However, your candles shouldn't be putting streams of noticeable black smoke into the air. When this happens, it can damage walls, furnishing, and fabrics.

You might have to troubleshoot a little to find the culprit for your overly smoky candles. The first place you'll want to look is the wick. A wick that is too large for the candle will produce an excessive amount of smoke. The solution for this is to switch to a smaller wick that is appropriate for the size of your candle.

Going overboard on fragrance oils can also cause your candles to produce some smoke. And sometimes, the solution doesn't have anything to do with the construction of the candle, but rather how it's being burned. Keep your wicks trimmed, and keeping your candles away from open windows and drafts, will help reduce smokiness.

Miscellaneous Tips

- There's no need to get rid of leftover wax. You can re-melt it and use it again as long as it hasn't been contaminated. It will come in handy the next time you make candles. Just keep a small container nearby and pour your unused wax into that before it hardens. This will greatly simplify the cleanup process. Containers like old egg cartons, milk cartons or cans work well for holding unused wax. Once the wax has cooled and hardened, remove it from the container and place it in a bag for future use. Label the bag with the type of wax and any additives for future reference.

- So can you do the same thing with old candle stubs? Say you've saved all the stubs from the candles that you've already burned and are planning to repurpose them into a brand-new candle. From an ecological and economical point of view, this is a great idea. After all, why waste perfectly good wax when it can just be remelted? The problem with this is that these stub collections usually contain bits of different types of waxes with different types of dyes and fragrances added in. This presents a major issue for wicking, not to mention the guessing game that ensues if you want to add additional colors or scents. So, what's the final answer? It's OK to experiment with old candle stubs, but do so with the understanding that you're probably not going to get optimal results. If you want to practice with them, that's fine, but candle stubs shouldn't be used when you're after high-quality results.

- Don't add unapproved items to your candles. We touched upon this briefly earlier, but it's important not to add anything to your candles that could interfere with the setting process or how they burn once lit. It's acceptable to use inert items for decorative purposes, like small pebbles, shells or coffee beans, because these types of things aren't going to affect the quality of wax or how well the wick performs. However, items like crayons, food colorings, and perfumes/colognes can destroy the integrity of your candle—and even make it dangerous due to the flammability factor. If you're unsure, ask yourself if the item you're thinking about adding could potentially melt into or infuse the wax. If the answer is yes and it didn't come from a candle making supplier, it's best to just say no.

- Don't take shortcuts. There really isn't any way to speed the candle making process along and still end up with the results you're looking for. Shortcuts like melting wax in the microwave or placing freshly poured candles in the refrigerator or freezer are never a good idea. The thing to keep in mind is that there are actual chemical and structural changes that occur during candle making. If you use a microwave or melt wax over too-high heat, you increase the chance of the wax melting unevenly or possibly burning in spots. This can cause problems when your candles are hardening and affect the overall appearance of the finished product. Speeding along the hardening process is also going to cause problems. Candle wax that hardens too quickly or is exposed to drastic changes in temperature becomes structurally weak and is predisposed to cracking and breaking.

- Give candle making your undivided attention. Do you have kids running around the house, a neighbor who likes to drop by unexpectedly, or a habit of picking up your phone every time you hear a ping? Candle making requires your undivided attention, so set aside some time when you know distractions will be at a minimum—and put your phone in a different room or turn it off to avoid temptation. Candle making is the perfect way to unplug, unwind and indulge in the exploration of your creative side, so give it the attention that it deserves.

- Always trim your candles after they've been lit. Just trim away the burnt part so that the candle looks clean and new again, then put it away for next time.

- To clean your candle jars and containers, you can get a soy-based cleaner. Made out of soybean oil, this is fragrance- and chemical-free, and its pleasant natural scent won't cause any breathing problems.

- If you think that your candle is too big for your purposes, then you can cut it in half. All you need to do is heat a knife over the flame for two seconds. You'll love how easy this makes cutting the candle.

- You may have heard that freezing candles will make them last longer, but that's just a myth. Freezing is only useful when you're having trouble taking a candle out of a mold. Its lifespan depends upon the type of wax, the wick, and its total size. As you burn the candle, it starts to melt no matter what temperature it was, to begin with.

- When you blow out a candle, it creates a lot of smoke, which isn't ideal—it's irritating to the eyes and the lungs. What you can do instead is to drop some melted wax onto the flame. The candle will go out smoothly, without any smoke or smell.

- You've probably seen candles that don't drip. Well, there are ways to make these dripless candles at home. If you use a thick wick right in the center, the candle will not drip on the surface and the area will stay clean. The type of wick may make some difference, but the thickness is the key. Thicker wicks also wick more efficiently and last longer. You also have to smooth the edges of the candle to ensure that it will be dripless.

- Don't worry if the candle flame isn't pointing straight up. Sometimes it will stay put, but it will move around if there is any pressure from the air from the side. There's nothing wrong with the candle; it's just the air controlling the flame.

CONCLUSION

The techniques in this book cover the basics, but there is an incredible world of candle making out there for you to explore. I recommend spending some time in your favorite candle and craft store and then spending a leisurely afternoon perusing all the different candle making ideas that you'll find online.

Your first few candles will probably be a little basic, and this is fine. First, there's absolutely nothing wrong with a simple, basic candle—in fact, they're quite beautiful. However, once you've gotten the basics mastered, you'll have the confidence to explore more advanced techniques.

For instance, you might want to experiment with creating purposefully mottled candles, or maybe adding ice to your wax, which creates tiny holes in your candle, similar to lace. You can also whip candle wax while it's cooling and then use the whipped wax to create decorative candles—like for peppermint scented, fluffy snowball candles, as a topping for a cupcake candle, or even a little dollop of "whipped cream" on a coffee scented container candle in a mug. The sky really is the limit.

Over time, you may find that you become bolder in how you mix fragrances to achieve new scents. You might like the idea of adding tiny pinecones to a large spruce scented pillar candle, or a mixture of lavender and geranium to a container candle that's infused with dried rose petals—perfect for relaxing on home spa day.

Whether your candle making hobby fills your own home with the soft glow of gorgeous candles, or you give them as gifts or even sell them for a profit, candle making is a rich, rewarding experience that you're going to love. Each one of your candle creations is infused with the loving energy you put into it. I am excited to welcome you to the wonderful world of candle making, and I know that you're going to enjoy it every bit as much as I have over the years.

ALSO BY
JOSEPHINE SIMON

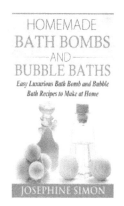

Image Credits

A Brief History
By https://wellcomecollection.org/works/mv7rkcm6 CC-BY-4.0, CC BY 4.0, https://commons.wikimedia.org/w/index.php?curid=36562708

Paraffin
By Gmhofmann [CC BY-SA 3.0 (https://creativecommons.org/licenses/by-sa/3.0)], from Wikimedia Commons

Double boiler
By Veganbaking.net from USA (Double Boiler) [CC BY-SA 2.0 (https://creativecommons.org/licenses/by-sa/2.0)], via Wikimedia Commons

Molds
By WillieWax [CC BY-SA 3.0 (https://creativecommons.org/licenses/by-sa/3.0)], from Wikimedia Commons

Made in the USA
Las Vegas, NV
10 March 2023